# Crows

# Crows

## A Carolrhoda Nature Watch Book

by Sylvia A. Johnson

Carolrhoda Books, Inc. / Minneapolis

*This book is for all my friends who are fascinated by crows and want to know their story.*

*The author would like to thank Kevin McGowan, research associate at the Cornell University Laboratory of Ornithology, and Carolee Caffrey, science associate at the National Audubon Society, for their assistance in the preparation of this book.*

Carolrhoda Books, Inc.
A division of Lerner Publishing Group
241 First Avenue North
Minneapolis, MN 55401 U.S.A.

Website address: www.lernerbooks.com

Library of Congress Cataloging-in-Publication Data

Johnson, Sylvia A.
  Crows / by Sylvia A. Johnson.
    p.   cm
  A Carolrhoda nature watch book.
  Includes index.
  ISBN: 1–57505–628–3 (lib. bdg. : alk. paper)
  1. Salmon—Juvenile literature.  I. Title.
QL696.P2367J64 2005
598.8'64—dc22                           2004000564

Manufactured in the United States of America
1 2 3 4 5 6 – JR – 10 09 08 07 06 05

# CONTENTS

Left: *Sometimes, it seems that crows are everywhere.*
Right: *The American crow is the most common corvid in North America.*

# CROWS ALL AROUND US

Crows have attracted the attention of humans for hundreds of years. People in some societies feared these big black birds because they associated them with evil and death. Other people respected crows as representatives of powerful spirits of nature. Farmers have usually seen crows as a threat to their crops.

In recent years, people in cities throughout North America and other parts of the world have become very familiar with crows. The birds have made themselves at home in modern urban and suburban surroundings. They can be seen—and heard—in backyards and city parks, at shopping malls, and on golf courses. Crows are all around us.

The crows that hang out in your backyard belong to a family of birds called Corvidae (KOR-vih-dee). Members of this scientific family are generally known as **corvids** (KOR-vihds). There are about 118 **species,** or kinds, of corvids, and they can be found on every continent except Antarctica. North America is home to 20 species of this family of birds.

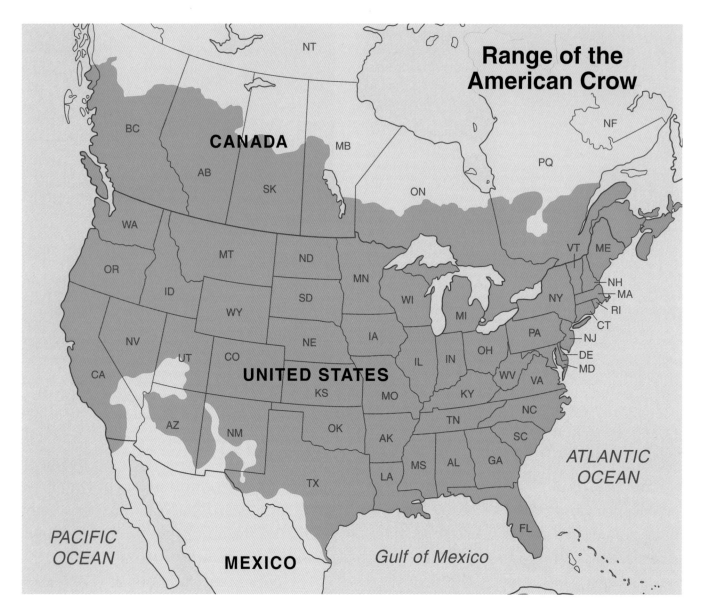

**Range of the American Crow**

The American crow is probably the most common of the North American corvids. It lives in almost all parts of the United States and Canada. This bird has features typical of many members of the Corvidae family—a stout body, strong legs and beak, and shiny black feathers.

The fish crow is a smaller North American crow species usually found along the eastern coast of the United States. Northwestern crows live along the northwestern coast. Two other crow species make their homes in Mexico.

The common raven, another well-known corvid, is larger than the American crow. Crows usually measure 17 to 21 inches (45–55 centimeters) from head to tail, while ravens may be as much as 27 inches (70 cm) in length. A crow's wingspan is about 3 feet (0.9 meters). A raven may have a wingspan of 4 feet (1.2 m). Ravens are found in many parts of North America, as well as in Europe and Asia. In the eastern half of the United States, they usually live in rugged, uninhabited regions, but in the western part of the country and in Canada, ravens are often found in cities, just as crows are.

*The common raven is larger than the American crow.*

Magpies are corvids with long, sweeping tails. Many magpies in western North America and northern Europe and Asia have elegant black and white feathers. Magpies in tropical regions may be dressed in emerald green or sapphire blue feathers.

Other colorful members of the Corvidae family are the jays. The bright blue feathers of the blue jay are a common sight in many parts of North America. Other jays with blue feathers are the scrub jays. One species lives in Florida, while two others are found in the western United States. Green jays live in the southern parts of Texas, as well as in Mexico and Central America. These vivid birds have blue and black feathers on their heads and beautiful shades of green on their bodies.

Above: *This western scrub jay holds an egg that it stole from another bird's nest.*
Above right: *The blue jay is another familiar and noisy corvid.*
Right: *The magpie, with its black and white feathers and long tail, is common in the western United States.*

If you have ever gone camping in the northern or western forests of North America, you've probably met the gray jay. This jay, known as the camp robber, is a bold bird that seems to know just what it wants and how to get it. These are qualities it shares with crows and other members of the Corvidae family.

Of all the corvids, the American crow is probably the most familiar to people in the United States and Canada. In this book, we will take a look at the life and habits of the American crow.

Left: *Green jays live in Texas and Mexico.*
Right: *The gray jay hangs around campsites looking for food.*

*Many crows live in rural areas.*

# COUNTRY BIRD, CITY BIRD

Ever since the late 1950s, more and more American crows have been moving from rural to urban and suburban areas. The same thing has been happening with other species in Europe and Asia. Scientists believe that crows are moving because of changes in the environment.

Crows in the country make their homes in large open areas with scattered trees. The birds usually find food in fields and pastures. Crows are **omnivorous** (ohm-NIV-uhr-us), which means that they eat just about anything. Their diet includes seeds, nuts, fruits, insects, worms, mice, small reptiles, bird eggs, baby birds, and dead animals.

Crows in rural areas also eat grains growing in the field, such as corn and wheat. In the past, farmers put scarecrows in their fields to frighten away hungry crows. These figures were supposed to look like humans guarding the crops. They didn't fool the crows for very long or prevent them from making a meal in a cornfield.

When it's time for mating and nesting, country crows seek out trees in the areas where they live. They build stick nests high up in tall trees, usually at the edges of woodlands. Crows also **roost** (gather in large groups) in trees during the fall and winter, after nesting season is over.

*Farmers dislike crows because they often raid their cornfields.*

*City parks have large trees, open areas, and lots of discarded food—all the things that crows like.*

The large trees that crows need for roosting and nesting are no longer as common in rural areas as they were in the past. Forests and woodlands have been cut down to make space for farms or for housing developments. Some of the largest trees still surviving are found not in the country, but in cities and suburbs. These big trees are in parks and cemeteries, on golf courses and college campuses, even in people's yards. Crows have discovered that city trees make good places for nesting and roosting.

The birds have also learned that food is often plentiful in urban surroundings. They can find lots of insects and worms in people's lawns and in the grassy areas of parks and golf courses. Other sources of food are roadkill and garbage.

Squirrels and other animals killed by cars can be found on city streets. There are also trash cans and dumpsters, even landfills, overflowing with rotting food. Crows are very fond of **carrion** (dead, rotting meat), and city garbage provides a feast for them.

Another possible advantage to city life is increased safety. In the country, a crow's biggest enemy is the great horned owl, a large **predator** that kills both young and adult crows for food. This sharp-eyed hunter sees much better in the dark than crows do. Great horned owls are not common in most cities. If an owl does come near a roost in the city, artificial lights along streets and in parks and parking lots make it easier for crows to spot the predator.

*In the city, crows can find roadkill to eat* (above) *and avoid their greatest enemy, the great horned owl* (above right).

*Some states hold special hunting seasons for crows living in rural areas.*

In the city, crows are also protected from another dangerous predator—humans. Even though studies show that corvids eat many insects that damage farmers' crops, crows in the country have always been considered pests. People have shot or poisoned crows whenever they had a chance. Crows roosting in trees have even been blown up with dynamite. In 1972, crows were added to a federal law protecting birds that **migrate** (move from one region to another during the year). Killing crows became illegal. Since then, some states have held special hunting seasons for crows. They can be shot in certain areas at certain times of year, just as ducks and geese are. In the city, however, it is never legal to shoot crows—or any other birds. City parks and yards provide a safe refuge from human hunters as well as from owls.

There are still plenty of crows in the country, but populations in urban and suburban areas have been growing. Because crows are able to adapt quickly to new situations, more and more of them are learning that city life has a lot of advantages. In their new city surroundings, crows go about the normal business of being crows.

Because so many American crows are now living in urban areas, scientists have been able to get a closer look at these clever corvids. Researchers use wing tags and colored leg bands to mark young crows for identification. These marks allow them to recognize individual crows and follow their activities over many years.

Two researchers who have been studying city crows for several years are Carolee Caffrey of the National Audubon Society and Kevin McGowan of the Laboratory of Ornithology at Cornell University. As a result of their work, we have learned many fascinating things about the lives and habits of American crows.

*Crows have learned that they can be safer and find more food living in a city.*

17

*Crows often live together in family groups.*

## ALL IN THE FAMILY

Have you ever noticed that you don't often see a crow by itself? If there is one crow around, there will probably be two or three or even more. Many of the small groups of crows that you see are families. Just like most human families, American crow families are made up of parents and their offspring of different ages

It is very unusual for animal parents and their offspring to stay together. Most birds—for example, robins and chickadees—have no contact with their young after the young birds leave the nest. American crow families stay together so that the older offspring can help their parents to raise younger brothers and sisters. This system of raising young is called **cooperative breeding.**

Cooperative breeding is very rare in the animal world. Only about 3 percent of all animal species, including birds, raise their young in this way. In the family Corvidae, cooperative breeding is more common than in many other families of birds. In North America, the Florida scrub jay, the Mexican jay, and the brown jay, as well as the American crow, are all cooperative breeders.

Because they live in family groups, American crows usually mate for life. Only if one member of a pair dies or is unable to reproduce will the other bird look for a new mate. In most species of birds, males and females find new mates each year. Other birds that mate for life are ravens, swans, and geese.

*Unlike crows, the male and female robin have all the work of caring for their young. The adult birds have no contact with the young after they leave the nest.*

*Male and female crows mate for life and go through a period of courtship every spring.*

When breeding time comes in spring, crows usually go through a period of **courtship,** even if a male and female have been partners for many years. The two birds sit close together on a branch. They **preen** each other, with one bird running a beak through the feathers on the other's head, neck, or back.

After several weeks of courtship, the pair makes a nest. Crows build new nests each year. They never use old ones. When a male and female crow start nest building, some of their offspring from the previous year and even several years before that may assist them by collecting sticks and grass. Constructing the nest, however, is mainly the job of the female.

A crow's nest is usually built in the fork between tree branches about 65 feet (20 m) above the ground. It is large and bulky, with an outer layer of sticks and a middle layer of mud and grass. Inside is a lining made of soft materials, such as shredded bark, animal fur, moss, or twine. After the nest is completed, the male and female crow mate, and the female begins to lay her eggs. Most female crows lay from two to six eggs, one each day. After most of the eggs are laid, the female begins **incubating** them—sitting on the eggs to keep them warm. Like many female birds, an incubating female crow develops a featherless **brood patch** on the underside of her body. This bare area of skin is filled with a lot of blood vessels, which helps to transfer the female's body heat to the eggs.

*Female crows lay two to six eggs in their large nests.*

A female crow incubates her eggs for about 19 days. Her mate and the pair's young helpers bring insects, worms, and other food to the female while she is on the nest.

The male crow also guards his mate and their eggs. He watches for predators and for other male crows that might try to sneak in and mate with his partner.

*Young crows hatched in previous years help their parents feed the new nestlings.*

When the eggs hatch, the parent crows' work really gets tough. Crow chicks, like many other young birds, are completely helpless. They are blind, have no feathers, and are unable to feed themselves. The parent birds have to keep the babies warm and supply them with an almost endless amount of food.

Crow parents are lucky because they have assistants to help care for their **nestlings.** Although the female alone has the job of keeping the babies warm, her mate and the couple's older offspring work at bringing food.

*The nestlings have to depend on the adult crows for food.*

When the helpers approach the nest, the nestlings open their beaks wide, begging to be fed. The mouths of adult crows are black inside, but a young crow's mouth has a pink lining. This pink color seems to send a message to other crows, letting them know that the young need food.

A bird bringing food to the nest carries it in its **crop,** a kind of pouch inside its throat. The feeding bird puts its beak deep inside a nestling's mouth. Then it brings up small pieces of insects, worms, and other food stored in its crop and passes them on to the baby crow. As the nestlings get older, the adults may kill small birds and tear them up to feed to the young crows.

*The nestlings open their mouths when an adult approaches with food. The mouths of young birds have a pink lining, perhaps to show that they need food.*

*Crows will gather in groups to frighten off an enemy, such as this great horned owl.*

The crow family works together to defend its nest against hawks, owls, raccoons, and other animals that might attack the young. If family members see a predator in the area, they give a loud warning call. Often other crows will hear the call and come to join in **mobbing** the predator.

When crows mob a hawk or owl, they swoop around it, making loud cries and diving down at their enemy. They don't often make physical contact, but all the noise and confusion usually drives the predator away. Crows will sometimes mob dogs and cats or even people if they think that their young are being threatened. Researchers Carolee Caffrey and Kevin McGowan are often mobbed when they climb up to nests to mark young crows for identification and tracking.

*When the baby crow has most of its feathers, it is called a fledgling.*

Protected and fed by their parents, brothers, and sisters, young crows remain in the nest for about five weeks. By four weeks, they have most of their feathers, although the long feathers on their wings and tails continue to grow. When they are 5 weeks old and their wing feathers are longer, the young leave the nest and begin flying. At this point, they are **fledglings.** The young crows will be fed by their relatives for 6 to 8 more weeks, while they learn how to get their own food.

Fledging crows are very curious about their new surroundings. They test out all kinds of things to see if they are good to eat or to play with. Juvenile crows like playing with such objects as sticks, feathers, and bones. Researcher Kevin Mc-Gowan has had reports of crows tearing windshield wipers off cars. Crows of all ages also seem to play games. Carolee Caffrey has seen crows swing upside down from branches and play tug of war with grass or twigs. One crow in her study area slid down a grassy slope on top of a flattened plastic cup, and then another family member copied the trick.

While young crows explore their world and learn how to find food, most stay close to their families. Even after they can feed themselves, they usually don't leave home. Some crows stay with their parents for 5 years or more before going out on their own. Female crows do not mate and produce young until they are at least 2 years old. Males may be 4 or 5 before they have a family.

*Some young crows stay with their parents for many years before going out on their own.*

*A male crow guards his territory, the area in which a crow pair breeds and raises its young.*

One reason for this long delay is the need for a **territory,** a special area in which a pair of crows can breed and raise young. Without a territory, crows can't begin the job of reproduction. Finding a good territory may not be easy. The area must have an ample supply of food and places to roost and make nests. It can't be occupied by other pairs of crows. Crow territories are fairly large. In the city, the territory of a single pair may be 10 acres (4 hectares). Territories in the country are much larger.

Crows find territories in many ways. Sometimes a young crow may be able to settle on part of its parents' territory if the area is large enough to be divided. A crow might also get a territory by forming a partnership with a bird whose mate has died. Sometimes a male crow will move in with an older brother and help to raise his young. When the first brother dies, the second one inherits the territory.

Until they do find places of their own, young crows usually don't go far from home. They may leave for days or even weeks at a time, but they come back frequently to visit the family. When next year's breeding season arrives, they will be ready to help out at the nest, just like their older brothers and sisters.

*Until they find a territory, young crows usually stay near their family.*

*Some crows migrate to warmer places during the winter, but many stay near home.*

# CROWS IN WINTER

When summer is over, a crow family is ready for a change of scene. Some families may move far away from their home territory. Crows that live in very cold climates usually migrate to warmer places in the winter. For example, crows that live in parts of central Canada where the average January temperature is 0° F (−18° C) may move south to Kansas, Nebraska, or Oklahoma.

In regions where the winter is not so cold, crow families stay at home. They spend some time in their territories each day. At night, they usually move to roosts (places to rest and sleep) along with hundreds, thousands, or even millions of other crows. Crows that migrate also join roosts at night.

*On winter evenings, crows head to gathering places, where they call, chase each other, and look for food.*

Crows usually roost in patches of woodland where there are large trees and some thick undergrowth. Roosts are often located near open spaces—fields or even parking lots. A roost may be used for years and then suddenly be abandoned as crows move to another area.

If you watch the sky in autumn or winter as night begins to fall, you may see crows flying to their roosts. At first, the birds head for gathering places near the roost. They come in small groups to these "staging areas," where they spend time looking for food, chasing each other, and calling. When darkness comes, the birds fly off from the different staging areas, cawing loudly. Then they head for their roost, where they settle down into the trees.

Crows at a roost often spend the night quietly "chattering" with each other rather than sleeping. At dawn, they fly off to look for food. They will come back to the same roost each night until spring, when they return to their territories.

Crows are not the only birds to sleep in roosts. Robins, starlings, swallows, and blackbirds also form large roosts. Scientists believe that roosting together may help to protect birds from their enemies. With hundreds of birds in one place, a predator will have a hard time making a sneak attack.

*As the sun sets, the crows take off for roosting places, where thousands of crows may gather.*

*Crows spend the night in a winter roost. When morning comes, the birds will fly off to search for food.*

Crows in cities often roost in trees near brightly lit parking lots or shopping malls, so they can see predators more easily. If an owl or other predator does attack, each individual bird within a large group has less chance of being killed than if it were in a small group or by itself.

Researchers think that there may be other reasons why crows gather at roosts. Roosting together may allow individuals to share information about winter food sources. A bird that has had problems finding food might spot some well-fed crows at a roost. When the roost breaks up in the morning, the hungry crow could follow its more successful companions to the area where they have been feeding. A roost might also serve as a kind of crow social club. Young crows that are looking for mates might be able to check out possible partners at these winter gathering places.

*Crow families communicate with a range of rattles, clicks, coos, and caws.*

# CROW LANGUAGE

Like many other species of birds, crows use sounds to communicate with one another. Along with robins, wrens, finches, chickadees, and many other species, crows are considered songbirds. Most people don't find a crow's calls very musical, but the calls mean something to other crows.

Researchers studying crow communi-

cation know that these corvids make many kinds of sounds. In addition to the loud caws that humans usually hear, the birds produce a whole range of softer calls that sound like rattles, clicks, coos, and gurgles. These noises seem to be used in communications among crows that are close together, perhaps members of the same family.

Young crows, for example, have a begging call that they use to ask for food. It sounds something like *waaawwwwww.* After they leave the nest, the young make this call a lot to tell their parents and the helpers that they need to be fed. A female crow that is incubating eggs uses this same begging call. She is sending her family the same message—"I need food, and I can't get it for myself."

*An almost-grown crow still asks for food with a begging call.*

*Crows use loud caws to warn intruders and send long-distance messages.*

Crows seem to use the loud cawing calls to send long-distance messages. For example, these caws might mean "There is a predator in the area. Come and join in a mob." Or "Watch out! You're trespassing in my territory." An individual crow often has its own special version of these calls. Researchers think that members of a crow family can probably identify relatives by their calls.

Like most other corvids, crows are good **mimics.** They copy the calls and songs of other birds and make them part of their own language. Corvids sometimes copy sounds from the human world too. One raven living at an animal rehabilitation center imitated cell phones ringing and voices paging the center's staff. The bird had to be moved because it was causing so much confusion.

Crows that have been kept as pets often copy the words of their companions. These captive corvids may imitate human language in an attempt to communicate with their human family. A young crow taken from a nest when it is a few weeks old will **imprint** on its human captors. It develops the same strong bond with people as it would with other crows. Imitating the special language of humans may be a part of this connection.

If you think that having a pet crow might be fun, you should know that it is illegal to keep crows or other wild birds as pets. Scientists who capture young crows and raise the birds to study them need special permission from state and federal governments to do this.

*This young orphan crow is being cared for at the Wildlife Rehabilitation Center of Minnesota. When the young crow is able to care for itself, it will be released back into the wild.*

*In Europe, black crows were thought to be the associates of witches*

## CROWS AND PEOPLE

Whether crows are gathering in winter roosts or making nests in backyard trees, they are hard to ignore. Throughout most of human history, people have noticed crows. They have not always been pleased by what they have seen.

In the past, many societies thought of crows and ravens as birds of death. Because they feed on carrion, people often saw them around battlefields and other places where there were dead bodies. In Europe, the jet-black crow and raven, like the black cat, were also associated with witches and witchcraft.

Other beliefs about corvids were more positive. Many people in Europe and other parts of the world thought that crows could indicate future events. According to an old rhyme that is still heard, seeing one crow means sorrow in the future, while two crows predict joy. Three crows mean marriage, four mean birth, and so on. This rhyme, which goes back at least to the 1600s in Europe, was originally about counting magpies. When it was brought to North America, crows became the corvids that could point to the future.

Crows and ravens have had a special place in Native American cultures. They often represent spirits of nature and are considered sacred by many American Indian cultures. Among native peoples of northwestern North America, Raven is the powerful spirit that created human beings and gave them fire. But he also likes to play tricks on people and get them into trouble. Crow also has been seen as a trickster by some Native American peoples. Bold, greedy, and clever, Crow often makes mischief for humans, though sometimes helps them to solve their problems too.

*Native American people of the Northwest consider Raven a powerful spirit and have carved his likeness into totem poles* (left).

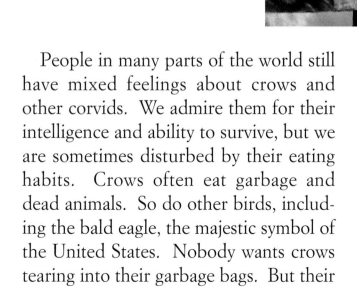

Left: *Because crows are scavengers, they help to keep city streets clean.*
Below: *This crow seems to be guarding a city bird feeder from other hungry birds.*

People in many parts of the world still have mixed feelings about crows and other corvids. We admire them for their intelligence and ability to survive, but we are sometimes disturbed by their eating habits. Crows often eat garbage and dead animals. So do other birds, including the bald eagle, the majestic symbol of the United States. Nobody wants crows tearing into their garbage bags. But their eating small animals killed on roads and highways helps to keep cities clean. Crows and other **scavengers** play an important role in the balance of nature.

Crows also eat the eggs and young of other birds. Crows are predators, just like owls, hawks, lions, sharks—and humans. Killing other animals for food is part of a predator's natural way of life. While we may not like the idea, we can't blame the crows for doing what comes naturally to them.

Because crows are becoming more common in cities, some people believe that their eating habits threaten backyard songbirds. Crows do prey on small songbirds, such as robins and cardinals, but so do raccoons, cats, and other animals. The crow is only one of the many dangers that threaten songbirds. A more serious threat to many species of North American songbirds is the destruction of forests in Central and South America, where these birds spend the winter.

People have had another reason to be concerned about crows. The birds have been connected with the spread of the West Nile virus. This virus was originally found in Africa and the Middle East. In 1999, it appeared in North America, when large numbers of dead crows were found in New York State. Studies showed that the birds had been infected by the virus, which had attacked their brains. After its initial appearance, West Nile virus moved slowly through the United States. By late 2003, it had reached 46 states. Its spread was marked by the deaths of hundreds of crows, blue jays, and other birds.

*Crows can't be blamed for eating garbage and attacking smaller birds. These habits are part of their natural way of life.*

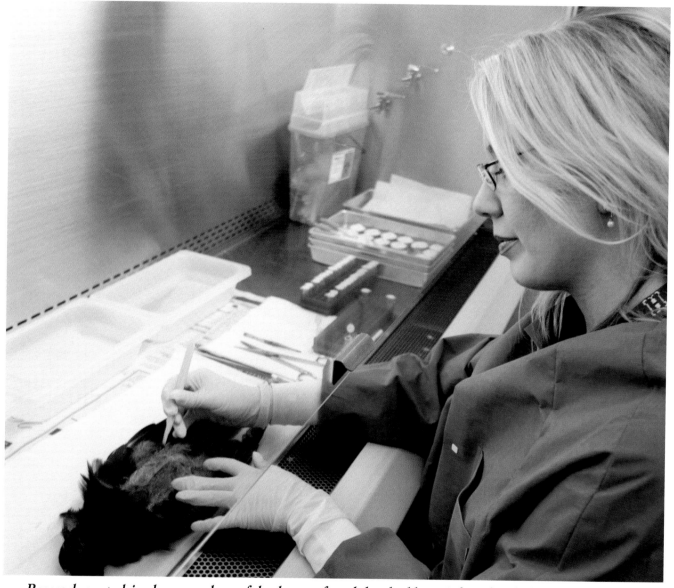

*Researchers studying large numbers of dead crows found they had been infected with the West Nile virus.*

Researchers discovered that corvids and other birds are one part of the basic life cycle of West Nile virus. Mosquitoes are the other part. The insects pick up the virus by biting infected birds. Then they pass it on when they bite other birds. Many kinds of birds can carry West Nile virus in their bodies without being harmed. Members of the Corvidae family, however, seem to be seriously affected by the virus.

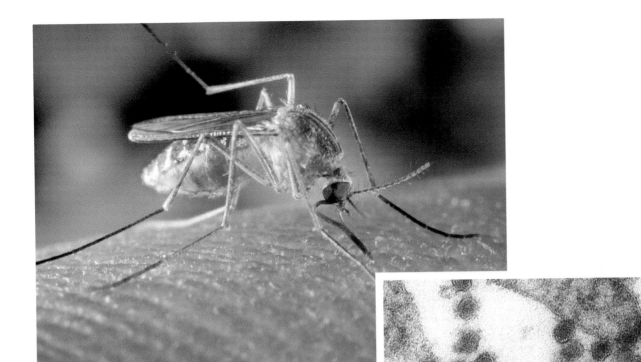

*Certain kinds of mosquitoes carry the West Nile virus* (right) *from bird to bird and sometimes to humans.*

West Nile virus is kept alive by being passed back and forth between mosquitoes and birds. If a mosquito carrying the virus happens to bite a human or another animal, however, they can also become infected. Scientists call these "incidental infections." Since 1999, more than 13,000 people in the United States have been infected by West Nile virus. About 500 people have died from diseases caused by the virus, but most have not developed any serious symptoms. Other animals that have been infected are horses, cats, chipmunks, and domestic rabbits.

In the case of West Nile virus, crows are not the bad guys they might first seem to be. They may be infected but they cannot pass the virus on to humans or other animals. Mosquitoes are the only creatures that can transmit West Nile virus to people.

*Schoolchildren learn about crows at the Minnesota Zoo.*

After getting to know more about American crows, you may think that these birds have some things in common with humans. Both species are intelligent, curious, and good at communicating. Both live in families, take care of their relatives, and play games. Crows, like humans, are quick to learn new ways of finding food and places to live.

Having crows around us is something like living next door to a big, noisy family. Maybe we should get used to our new neighbors and learn to enjoy their company. It doesn't look as if the crows are going to move away anytime soon.

44

*Crows are good at communicating with each other, but bald eagles don't understand crow language.*

# GLOSSARY

**brood patch:** an area of featherless skin that develops on the underside of a female bird's body when she is incubating eggs

**carrion:** the rotting flesh of dead animals

**cooperative breeding:** a system of raising young in which parents are assisted by other family members

**corvids:** members of the family Corvidae. Crows, ravens, magpies, and jays are corvids.

**courtship:** a period before mating during which males and females form a bond. Courtship among birds often includes singing and mutual preening.

**crop:** a kind of pouch in a bird's throat, used to store food

**fledglings:** young birds that have developed the feathers necessary for flight

**imprint:** to learn to recognize other animals as close relatives. Young birds usually imprint on the first living creatures they see.

**incubating:** sitting on eggs to keep them warm

**migrate:** to travel between one place or climate to another. Many birds in North America fly to warmer regions in winter.

**mimics:** birds that can copy the calls of other birds or even human language

**mobbing:** birds joining together to drive an enemy away

**nestlings:** young birds in the nest

**omnivorous:** eating both plants and animals

**predator:** an animal that kills other animals for food

**preen:** to use the beak to clean and arrange feathers. Many species of birds preen both themselves and their companions.

**roost:** to gather together in one place to rest or sleep. Crows roost in large trees.

**scavengers:** animals that eat carrion

**species:** a group of living things that share many characteristics and can mate and produce healthy young

**territory:** an area in which an animal makes its home and hunts for food

# INDEX

# ABOUT THE AUTHOR

**Sylvia A. Johnson** has had a long and productive career as an editor and writer of award-winning books for young people. She has worked on publications about such different subjects as beekeeping, raptor rehabilitation, and the role of maps in human history. Doing research for her books, Sylvia has studied rare old maps in libraries, observed surgery on injured raptors, and put on coveralls and a veiled hat to get a close-up look at a beekeeper at work. Her research on American crows was conducted in her own backyard in Minneapolis, Minnesota, where she watched crows nesting and roosting in a neighbor's large trees. Hearing birds singing in her yard inspired another of her books in the Carolrhoda Nature Watch series, *Songbirds,* which explains just how birds sing and what important messages their songs carry. In addition to observing backyard birds, Sylvia enjoys reading, working in the garden, cooking Indian food, and traveling to Mexico and Central America to visit the ruins of ancient Mayan cities.

# PHOTO ACKNOWLEDGMENTS

The images in this book are reproduced through the courtesy of: © Steve Maslowski/Visuals Unlimited, p. 2; © Wernher Krutein/Photovault, pp. 4–5; © Stephen J. Krasemann/Photo Researchers, Inc., p. 6; © Rick & Nora Bowers/Visuals Unlimited, p. 7; © Ken M. Johns/Photo Researchers, Inc., p. 9; © Anthony Mercieca/Root Resources, p. 10 left, 25, 26; © Richard Day/Daybreak Imagery, pp. 10 upper right, 11 left; © G. C. Kelley/Photo Researchers, Inc., p. 10 lower right; © George D. Lepp/Photo Researchers, Inc., p. 11 right; © Todd Fink/Daybreak Imagery, p. 12; © Gary Zahn/Bruce Coleman, Inc., p. 13; © Rafael Macia/Photo Researchers, Inc., p. 14; State of Minnesota Department of Natural Resources, p. 15 top; © Maslowski/Photo Researchers, Inc., p. 15 bottom; © BillMARCHEL.com, p. 16; © Maslowski Wildlife Productions, pp. 17, 32, 33; © Art Wolfe/Photo Researchers, Inc., p. 18; © John Mitchell/Photo Researchers, Inc., p. 19; © Tim Zurowski/CORBIS, pp. 20, 34; © Scott Camazine/Photo Researchers, Inc., pp. 21, 23, 24; © Jim Zipp/Photo Researchers, Inc., pp. 22, 41; © Tom and Pat Leeson, pp. 27, 29, 39 left, 45; © Alan G. Nelson/Root Resources, p. 28; © Gregory K. Scott/Photo Researchers, Inc., pp. 30, 40 left; © Kenneth W. Fink/Root Resources, p. 31; © Dan Sudia/Photo Researchers, Inc., p. 35; © Tom Brakefield/SuperStock, p. 36; © Todd Strand/Independent Picture Service, p. 37; Mary Evans Picture Library, p. 38; © Joseph Sohm/ChromoSohm Inc./CORBIS, p. 39 right; © Frank W. Mantlik/Photo Researchers, Inc., p. 40 right; © Reuters NewMedia Inc./CORBIS, p. 42; Center For Disease Control And Prevention/Public Health Image Library, p. 43 both.© Annie Griffiths Belt/CORBIS, p. 44.

Front Cover: © Tim Zurowski/CORBIS.